Jungle Shorts

Irene Rawnsley

Illustrated by Tony Kerins

D0528207

OXFORD
UNIVERSITY PRESS

1

It was Friday afternoon. Class 3 had
put on their coats and were waiting in
a line to go home. Lenny was at the
back because the zip on his anorak had
stuck. He was so busy with the zip that
he nearly missed what Mr Cox the
teacher said.

'Here's a letter for you all,' said Mr Cox. 'Don't lose it and don't forget to give it to your parents. There's good news inside.'

Lenny wanted to know what the good news was. He rushed across the playground to meet his mum.

4

'Quick! Open this letter,' he said.
'Mr Cox says there's good news inside.'

'Say hello to me first!' laughed his
mum, but she opened the letter. She
read it and told him, 'Class 3 is going
to have football lessons. Next week.
The school will lend you some boots.'

'Wow!' shouted Lenny. 'Real football! I bet I score fifteen goals!'

His mum put the letter in her bag.

'What about a stripy shirt and socks? Can I have a real football strip?' begged Lenny.

'Wait and see,' said Mum.

At home Lenny couldn't get out of his anorak and his mum had to help him.

'I'm glad you didn't break the zip. I can't get you another coat until next month,' she said.

'I don't want a new coat,' said Lenny, 'but can I have a real football strip? Please?'

'Ask me after tea,' said his mum.

They had pancakes for tea with jam and apple. Pancakes were Lenny's favourite. But today he ate as fast as he could.

He put down his knife and fork with a clatter.

'You promised to talk about football things after tea,' he said.

Mum took Mr Cox's letter from
her bag.

'Each child will need an old T-shirt
and some socks,' she read.

'No real football things?' asked Lenny.

'I'm sorry, no. Except for shorts.
Mr Cox wants you all to have new
shorts. We'll go to the market tomorrow
to look for some.'

Lenny was not happy but he knew his mum. She had made up her mind and that was that. He looked at his photos of football stars. They looked great. 'I bet they always had a proper football strip,' he thought. 'I bet they didn't have to wear an old T-shirt.'

That night he lay awake thinking. He was going to make sure his mum bought football shorts. He wanted proper white football shorts. Then he knew he could score lots of goals.

2

After breakfast the next day they set
out to buy the new shorts. The market
was two streets away from where Lenny
lived. On the way they saw Ted and
Shane from Class 3. Ted and Shane
lived near Lenny. They were kicking a
ball about beside the road.

Shane slammed the ball over to him and Lenny kicked it back.

'Want to play?' called Ted.

'I can't, not now. I'm off with my mum to buy new football shorts.'

'We've got ours already,' Ted shouted back.

The market was very crowded.
Everyone was looking at the fruit and
vegetables piled high on the stalls.
There were shoes and clothes for sale
under stripy canvas roofs. One man
was selling shorts.

'Get your jungle shorts!' he shouted.

He was wearing a wide straw hat and an enormous pair of jungle shorts over his trousers. They had big green trees on with monkeys smiling at the top.

'Big or small, they don't cost much,' said the man.

'No thanks,' said Lenny. 'I'm going to start football lessons next week. I need real football shorts.'

He pulled at his mum's hand. They struggled through the crowds trying to find real football shorts. They found lots of shorts that were too big and a little white pair that was too small. When they did find a pair in Lenny's size they cost far too much money.

'We'll just have to get the jungle shorts,' said Mum. 'The colours are lovely. I'm sure you'll like them better than white ones.'

Lenny pulled a face. 'Oh, Mum!' he said. 'But – '

'No buts,' said his mum.

They went slowly back to the man
selling jungle shorts. The pile on his
stall had gone down a lot.

'I knew you'd come back. I put aside
a pair just for you,' said the man.

He held a pair of jungle shorts
against Lenny's trousers.

'A perfect fit!' he said with a smile.

Lenny's mum opened her purse and paid for the shorts. The man put them in a bag and handed it over.

'There you are, son. Have fun wearing them!'

Lenny did not smile. 'I wish they were real football shorts,' he said.

'Jungle shorts are the next best thing,' said his mum.

On the way home they saw Tessa
and Pam from Class 3 kicking a ball
against a fence. They lived at the top of
Lenny's street.

'We can't wait till Monday for
football,' said the girls. 'We've got
new shorts!'

'So have I,' said Lenny. But he didn't
open his bag to show them.

3

On Monday afternoon Class 3 were
waiting for their first football lesson.
Everybody was noisy and excited,
swinging their bags of football things.
Lenny was at the back with the jungle
shorts in his bag. He didn't want to put
them on.

Mr Cox carried a big box of boots
into the changing room. They spent
a long time finding boots to fit
everyone.

'Now, put on your football things
and be quick about it,' he said.

Lenny got changed in a corner
behind the door.

When they were all ready Mr Cox
shouted, 'Get in line, everyone!'

Lenny made sure he was at the
back again. He didn't want anybody
to see his jungle shorts and he hid
behind Ted. He looked down to see
what Ted was wearing and got a
surprise.

Ted was wearing jungle shorts as
well! Lenny nudged him in the back
and said, 'Your shorts are the same
as mine!'

'Yes,' said Ted, 'and the same as
Pam's and Tessa's and Shane's!'

It was true. All the friends from
Lenny's street were wearing jungle
shorts. Mr Cox smiled.

'Five children in the same shorts.
It must be a record!' he said

'And we all live in Lyon Street,' said Lenny.

'In that case you must all play for the same team. You can be the Lyon Street *Lions*.'

When Mr Cox had sorted out three more teams they went out to the playing field.

They played five-a-side football until home time. The *Lions* team beat all the others and Mr Cox said they were the champions. Lenny scored five goals.

In the changing room the children untied their muddy boots and put on their clothes.

'All kit must be washed and boots clean for next Monday,' said Mr Cox. 'Don't leave it for your mum. Do it as soon as you get home and then you won't forget.'

Lenny was the first to be ready and
he ran to meet his mum at the gate. He
told her about his five goals and the
Lyon Street *Lions*.

'We'd better go home quickly now,'
said Lenny. 'I have to clean my boots
and wash my shorts!'

And when Mr Cox drove home for
his tea later on, he smiled to himself.
On Lyon Street there were five pairs of
jungle shorts blowing on the washing
lines.

About the author

I live in the Yorkshire Dales and since I was little, I've always liked writing poems and stories. Nowadays, I write in a room overlooking fields and hills and I'm often joined by our black-and-white cats, Silver and  Fagley. Fagley was an abandoned kitten and he was named after the first bus that passed us on the way home.

My own children are grown-up now but I have two grandsons, Luke and Peter, who take a great interest in my books.